Living Things
and their changing
Habitats

First published 2020
Foxton Books
London, UK

Copyright © Foxton Books, 2020

ISBN: 978-1-83925-002-6

Written by Nichola Tyrrell
Designed by Maryke Goldie
Logo design: Stewart Wright (2Wright Design)
Cover design: Ed White
Education consultant: Frances Barlow

About Foxton Primary Science:

The Foxton Primary Science series supports Key Stage 1, Lower Key Stage 2
and Upper Key Stage 2 Science.

This title supports the Living Things and their Habitats section of **Lower Key Stage 2** Science
through a variety of features and **STEAM**-inspired tasks that cover all curriculum requirements.

Colourful, engaging content blends information with prompts
for further discussion and investigation.

Keywords, creative activities and quizzes reinforce comprehension,
along with challenging words (in bold) explained in the glossary.

Contents

Grouping living things

We know that living things include two main groups: animals and plants. We can put living things into more groups, depending on what they look like, how they behave and their habitat. Another name for any living thing is **organism**.

One way to group animals is by those that have backbones and those that do not.

Sheep have backbones.
They are **vertebrates**.

Sorting organisms into different groups is called **classifying**. We can classify plants into those that are flowering and those that are non-flowering.

non-flowering

flowering

Who is MRS NERG?

All living things have certain characteristics in common. There seven processes that all living things do:

Movement
Reproduction
Sensitivity (to their surroundings)
Nutrition (get or make food)
Excretion (get rid of waste from the body)
Respiration (release energy)
Growth

Both animals and plants have MRS NERG characteristics.

The animal kingdom

The two main groups into which scientists classify animals are vertebrates and invertebrates. Vertebrates are animals with a backbone.

We can classify vertebrates further into the following groups:

mammal

fish

bird

amphibian

reptile

Keywords backbone invertebrate vertebrate

There are more invertebrates than any other type of animal. More than 96 per cent of all the world's animal species are invertebrates.

centipede

beetle

Invertebrate animals do not have a backbone. An invertebrate's body is either soft, like a worm, or it has a hard covering, like a crab or beetle.

Invertebrates include many sea creatures, like starfish, and creepy crawlies such as spiders and insects.

starfish

Classifying animals

Take a walk through a local habitat and look for wildlife. This could be your back garden or school grounds, or a pond in a city park.

You will need:
camera or notebook and pencil

spider in its web

carpenter ants in a log

Check micro-habitats too, perhaps under a log or rock or in a puddle.

Take a photo or draw each creature that you spot. Include those you don't recognise and describe how they look.

Create a classification key like the one below to sort the animals by answering questions about how they look. Think about which questions you might put in the boxes to complete the key.

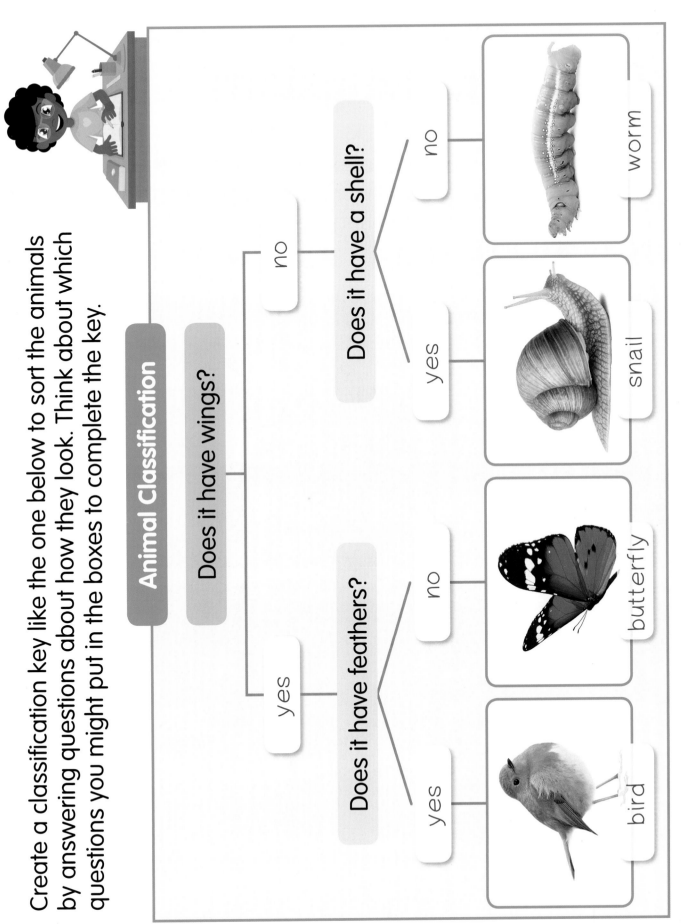

Animal Classification

Does it have wings?

yes   no

Does it have feathers?

yes   no

bird   butterfly

Does it have a shell?

yes   no

snail   worm

The plant kingdom

As with animals, we can classify plants into two main groups. Plants are either flowering or non-flowering. Most of the world's plants are flowering. Some flowering plants are trees and shrubs.

Deciduous trees, such as the maple, are giant flowering plants. They produce seeds, fruits and flowers.

maple tree

Keywords coniferous deciduous spore

Non-flowering plants are grouped into those that reproduce either with **spores** or seeds.

Spores are like tiny specks of dust. Thousands of these tiny **particles** are spread by wind or water. Most live in damp or shady areas as they need lots of water to survive.

fern spores

Ferns are plants that have spores on their leaves.

pine

Non-flowering plants that reproduce using seeds include coniferous trees like fir and pine.

We can also classify plants by the shape of their leaves.

Classifying plants

Investigate your area for examples of both flowering and non-flowering plants. Choose a few from each main group and make a picture to display. Group the plants by the **characteristics** they share.

Classify those that have flowers. Do you see any fruits or seeds?

For non-flowering plants, is your example seed-producing or spore-producing? How can you find out?

Try hand-printing to show leaves on a tree.

How many different plants did you find? Count both the flowering and non-flowering plants. Of which group did you find the most?

Materials you might use:

Add labels to your pictures. These may include:

- flowers
- leaves
- cones
- produces spores
- woody stem or trunk
- fruit

Habitats and seasons

Habitats are home to different living things in different seasons. In the plant world, some flowers bloom in spring and summer only. Some animals leave their homes and migrate to other parts of the world to find the climate that suits them best.

Bluebells appear only in spring.

bluebells

Keywords climate habitat season

blackthorn fruit

Many deciduous plants will grow their fruits only in autumn and winter, like the blackthorn.

We can group animals and plants by their habitats. Some living things like hot and dry conditions while others need a cool, shady **environment** to survive.

cacti

Canada geese

Cacti plants like a hot dry habitat. They store water in their stems.

Canada geese migrate from the cold Arctic winters for milder climates in the south.

Make a habitat diorama

Design and build a diorama, a 3-D scene showing the different living things that make their home in a particular habitat.

Which habitat will you choose?

Depending on your choice of habitat, you will need:

- small cardboard box (or make your own using pieces of card and tape)
- paint
- items to make plants and animals such as modelling clay, card cut-outs, twigs, stones
- glue

cardboard box

modelling clay　　　　paint

Habitat ideas:

- countryside hedgerow
- woodland pond
- city park
- tropical rainforest
- Arctic Ocean
- desert
- coral reef
- seaside

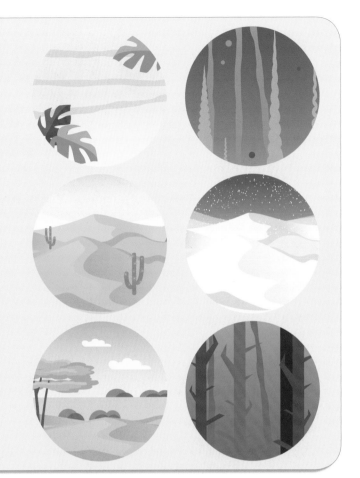

Changing habitats

An environment can change, affecting the living things that **inhabit** it. Some changes may happen naturally, such as a flooding or an earthquake. Other changes are man-made.

A tornado is a moving funnel-shaped wind storm that can destroy everything in its path.

tornado

Keywords destructive environment human impact

Humans can affect the environment and cause **negative** changes in habitats.

Littering is dangerous for wildlife.

Fumes from cars pollute the air we breathe.

Can you think of any other ways that humans affect the environment?

Building on land destroys habitats for plants and animals.

Protecting the environment

Not all human activity is dangerous for the environment. People around the world are working hard to help save, protect and **preserve** Earth's living things and its habitats.

Nature reserves help to protect plants and animals and ensure their habitat is safe.

This **orphaned** elephant calf in Kenya needs help feeding.

Keywords   preserve   recycling   waste

Cleaning rivers, lakes, ponds and seas will stop wildlife from eating plastic and getting tangled up in it.

recycling

Recycling plastic, paper and glass means less waste is buried in **landfills**.

Growing trees helps to rebuild woodland habitats.

newly planted trees

Don't litter!

Make a poster to remind people not to litter. Research and print out photos, or draw your own pictures.

Write on your posters the reasons why we should not litter:

Classify by habitat

Write a list of animals and classify them by their habitat, such as polar, woodland, coastal, tropical rainforest, savannah, desert.

Include vertebrates and invertebrates.

vertebrate

invertebrate

What other animals might share the rainforest with this monkey?

Which neighbours might this woodland hedgehog have?

23

Which habitat do earthworms prefer?

Earthworms live underground but do they prefer moist soil or dry soil? Does living in soil mean they don't like light? Try this experiment to find out what earthworms like. Make predictions before the experiment about what you think will happen.

You will need:

- container (shoe-box size)
- paper towels
- water
- earthworms (2–5)

earthworm

paper towels

shoe-box

1. Place a dry paper towel in the container, covering half of the bottom.

2. Place a wet paper towel on the other half.

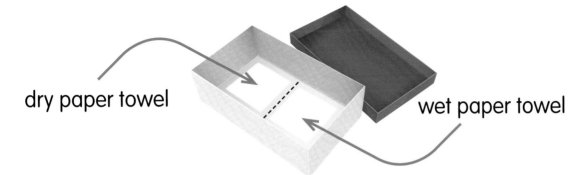

dry paper towel

wet paper towel

3. Put the earthworms in the middle of the container so they are touching both paper towels.

4. Observe the earthworms.
   Are they moving to one side or the other?

5. Place the lid on top of the container and wait.

6. After 20 minutes, check your earthworms.
   - Have they moved?
   - Are they on the wet paper or on the dry?
   - Is there anything else that you notice about them?

Now test your earthworms to see if they prefer different types of soil.

1. Empty your container and place a layer of soil, about 2 centimetres deep, in one half.

2. Place soil mixed with a few leaves, twigs or grass in the other half.

soil

mixed soil

3. Place the earthworms in the middle of the container and put on the lid.

4. After 20 minutes, check your earthworms.
   – If they have moved, where did they go?
   – Did they all move to the same area?

5. Make a chart to record your observations. Were your predictions correct?

Earthworm experiment observations

Name: _____ Date: _____

Testing preference for dry or wet conditions	Location of worms after 20 minutes
Wet paper	
Dry paper	
Overlapping papers	

Did the worms stay together?

Testing preference for plain or mixed soil	Location of worms after 20 minutes
Plain soil	
Mixed soil	

Did the worms stay together?

Just for fun:

Can you tell which end of the worm is the head? How many segments do the worms have?

! After experimenting, be sure to return the earthworms carefully to their natural habitat.

Comprehension check

1. What are the two main groups of animals?

2. What are the two main groups of plants?

3. Which animal group describes those with backbones?

4. Name the two groups missing from this list of vertebrate animals: mammals, amphibians, reptiles

5. True or false: there are more invertebrates on Earth than vertebrates.

6. Is an earthworm a vertebrate or an invertebrate?

7. True or false: deciduous trees are large flowering plants.

8. Are coniferous trees flowering or non-flowering plants?

9. Do ferns and mosses reproduce with spores or seeds?

10. Is an earthquake a natural change or a man-made change to the environment?

Turn to page 32 to mark your answers.

Vocabulary check

1. C _ _ _ _ _ _ _ _ _ _ is the sorting of organisms into different groups.

2. Another name for any living thing is o _ _ _ _ _ _ _ .

3. I _ _ _ _ _ _ _ _ _ _ _ do not have backbones.

4. M _ _ N _ _ _ describes the seven life processes of all living things.

5. Non-flowering plants reproduce either with s _ _ _ _ _ or seeds.

6. Canada geese m _ _ _ _ _ _ from the cold Arctic winters for milder climates in the south.

7. An e _ _ _ _ _ _ _ _ _ _ _ can change, affecting the living things that inhabit it.

8. To r _ _ _ _ _ _ is to reuse waste materials.

9. L _ _ _ _ _ is rubbish that is not in a bin.

10. Human i _ _ _ _ _ _ is the effect of people on the planet.

Turn to page 32 to mark your answers.

Glossary

Definitions relate to the context of word usage in this book.

characteristic – a quality that makes an animal or person different from others

classifying – the act of putting things into groups

coniferous – the type of tree that produces cones and needles; most are evergreen

deciduous – the type of tree that drops its leaves each year

environment – the conditions and things, such as climate and organisms, in an area

habitat – the natural home, or environment, of a plant or animal

inhabit – to live somewhere or in something as a home

invertebrate – an animal without a backbone or skeleton inside its body

investigate – to study and learn about something

landfill – a place where waste is buried in the ground

litter – rubbish that is not put in a bin or recycled

micro-habitat – a small habitat within a bigger one; a dead tree stump is a micro-habitat in a forest

moist – damp; slightly wet

negative – not helpful

organism – any living thing

orphaned – an animal or human child whose parents have died

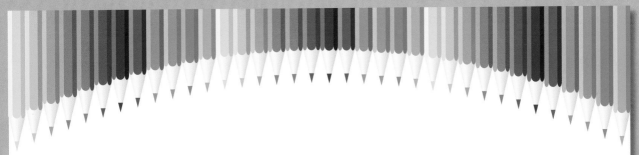

particle – a very tiny amount or small piece of something

prediction – a statement of what might happen in the future

preserve – to protect from harm

reproduce – to grow and have offspring or young

spore – a cell or group of cells that reproduce in some plants and animals

vertebrate – an animal with a backbone or skeleton inside its body

waste – rubbish

Index

Quiz answers

Comprehension check, page 28

1. vertebrates and invertebrates; 2. flowering and non-flowering;

3. vertebrates; 4. birds and fish;

5. true; 6. invertebrate; 7. true;

8. non-flowering; 9. spores; 10. natural

Vocabulary check, page 29

1. classifying; 2. organism; 3. invertebrates;

4. MRS NERG; 5. spores; 6. migrate; 7. environment;

8. recycle; 9. litter; 10. human

Photo credits

Shutterstock.com: Cover: Jan Martin Will; pp 1–2: Kazakova Maryia, robuart; pp 4–5: javarman, Sergey Mironov, PeJo, Ondrej Prosicky, Vectors bySkop; pp 6–7: Eric Isselee, MRS. SUCHARUT CHOUNYOO, Worraket, Vojce; pp 8–9: BlueRingMedia, Vadym Lesyk, Jeremy A. Casado, Jakkarin chuenaka, Aleksandar Dickov, girl-think-position, Butterfly Hunter, clarst5; pp 10–11: Elena Elisseeva, Lorelyn Medina, Irina Rogova, raulbaenacasado, Brandy McKnight; pp 12–13: PhotoUG, ValeryMinyaev, FamVeld, McLura; pp 14–15: Visharo, LianeM, Galyna Andrushko, Dennis W Donohue; pp 16–17: Iconic Bestiary, Kansitang Pittayanon, Luba Shushpanova, Dragon Images, cosmic_fellow, Lorelyn Medina, artbesouro; pp 18–19: Minerva Studio, Icswart, Paolo Bona, mbrand85, Iconic Bestiary; pp 20–21: Piu_Piu, Jose y yo Estudio, ITTIGallery, Callums Trees; pp 22–23: Orange Vectors, Om Yos, HappyPictures, Volodymyr Goinyk, Coatesy; pp 24–25: Lorelyn Medina, Mama Belle and the kids, Valentina Razumova, Cipariss, Flipser; pp 26–27: Lorelyn Medina, Nikolay Antonov, domnitsky, xpixel, Christos Georghiou; pp 28–29: GraphicsRF, pp 30–32:GraphicsRF, Olkita, Lorelyn Medina, Teguh Mujiono